Contents

Foreword

We are living in a wonderful world. Everything get more and more meaningful and transparent by the advantage of new technology and shared information. World changes and so does China even more speedily. No matter what your goal is, for tour / business or anything legal else, China is a magic and attractive land with great potential and opportunities due to its large territory and population.

During the past three decades, China changed a lot, not only in the visible appearance, but also in people's mind, so in order to keep  up with the step of changes, we need the latest update about China. I write this book according to my past experience and the knowledge I got from books and internet, adding a little of analysis and opinions after carefully thinking.

Many years ago, freedom of speech and writing

were severely limited and it's illegal to write books like I am doing now. It was considered as a betrayal of the nation. Thanks for this free sky now and wish everyone can breathe in the fresh and free air.

I hope this book can help you better understand China and guide you make right judgment and choice, which lead you to the success and happiness on this ancient and modern land.

About the author

Author of this book, me, Yisong zhang, ever tried in many fields and careers since 1995, and now I am an independent advertisement man engaging in propagandizing and popularizing the products or service for the local companies. My experience and thinking gave me my own view angle to look upon the world. I've been living in China for 40 years and as a common one in the country I want to record my thoughts according to the way which I think is right.

Thanks for your taking time to pass by and it may be what you need and are interested in. Enjoy yourself anytime!

1. General Situation

China is located in the east of Asia and the western shore of Pacific Ocean. Neck and neck with USA, China get a land area of 9,600000 square kilometers. But for the big population of 1.3 billion (one-fifth of the total of the whole world), land holdings per head average here is low. Most of the citizens are living in the eastern China where natural environment and economy development is better than that in the west of the country. Now the Chinese government is trying its best to change this unbalanced situation between the west and east.

China also has one of the earliest civilization and has a recorded history that dates from some 3500 years ago. "Zhonghua", the Chinese name for the country, means "central land," a reference to the Chinese belief that their country was the geographical center of the earth and the only true civilization. By the 19th century China had become a politically and economically weak nation, dominated by foreign powers, since 1840 the UK broke into by means of opium and gun .

So China could no more close the door and no longer last the unchanged comfortable days. That's a process full of sadness / hurt / shame and conflict. The old system of inside values and outside object were completely upside-down. People here got lost before new things and new thoughts.

During the next decades, the Chinese people searched their way for a better future. It's difficult and suffering to deny the past and build a new world. Reforming mind and values is much more difficult than reforming the real objects. It's like a severe brain storm to everyone and caused so much confusions and problems that these lead to the social instability and people suffered from this very much. Wars and conflicts were everywhere. Powerful forces competed on this land and there was full of death / blood / cheat and any kinds of bad things. The regulation of nature again was proved that a completely new world must be based on a completely destruction of the old world.

The day finally came in 1949. The founding of The People's Republic Of China announced the end of civil war and those chaotic days. A new page had been turned and new order started. The Communist Party grasped the control of the mainland and the KMT fled to the island of Taiwan. From then on, the channel of Taiwan became an endless and forever topic for Chinese people. Difference of ideology was emphasized and rendered to the extreme, especially in the mainland. People dressed in the same, spoke the same political catchwords, criticized and struggled to

the minority enemies, and so on. Those days were gray for those minorities many of whom in fact were talented people and got different opinions from the mainstream ideology. The Communist Party won the competition in the war field which just meant the warring days' end. There is a famous Chinese saying that power is easy to get but difficult to drive. The sun still raise and down, and people's life is still on day by day. Then another great challenge was in front of the Communist Party to cure the damaged country.

Mao zedong, a great name influenced several generations worldwide. His theory was accumulated in the warring period, which encouraged his people and helped him defeat his enemies. He was the savior and idol of the poor and the lower-leveled people. For nearly some thirty years' time, hot cult of Mao was popular in China. Class struggle was the No. 1 mission that laboring people need to keep eyes on the class enemies, and economic construction was ignored. Political fanaticism damaged the main body of the country and finally things were set right in 1978 after Deng xiaoping became the leader and began the policy of opening up.

Trouble times get further and further away from today. The abundant material life gradually waters down the memory of that period. Right or wrong, love or hate, all went with the wind. Time is the fairest judger and will keep on witnessing our world.

Author's points

We need a heading indicator when we lost the direction. China was ever a big testing site for different directions. We show the greatest respect to those persons whether they are great or not for their devotion on searching ways for people's happiness. Their experience whether failed or succeeded will both become a valuable fortune of   human being.

2. We are facing more and more challenges

2013 is the thirteenth year of the new century. The whole world is undergoing a deep revolution / development and readjustment since the financial crisis in 2008. New characters appears in many fields such as politic / economy / culture / science and security. Contrast of power changed to a new balance. We can no more use the old methods and thoughts  to deal with the new situation. Especially to China, more and more challenges is testing its old system and it must reform much in every detail of the nation.

People now care less about economic for we needn't worry about the basic living condition any more. When our lower needs is meet, we will think of things higher-level. In fact, the developing of economy caused new troubles and problems in political / social / moral field. World is an endless machine. When we think we get a destination, soon we find it's actually another new start. Challenges exist anywhere and anytime.

In China, there are 10 top challenges that everyone need to be careful and then we can avoid their negative effects.

Challenge No. 1 : Corruption exceeds the base line of the public

Corruption is dishonesty and illegal behavior by people in positions of authority or power.

People hate corruption. This is an unchanged rule everywhere. Just forty years ago, there is no corruption in China. it was a red world against all kinds of capitalism to carry out the real socialism. That's an extremely method to fight against the private ideas and corruption. It got the effect but all the people were poor in living, which was concluded to be wrong in the Deng xiaoping's theory.

We advocate liberation of thoughts now and private property is respected and protected by law, which is a completely contrary from Maoism. People no more trust the baseless political theories, but chase the real materials. Eager for money or power gradually become the main value of the society. Then

economy development became the center of everything. Few people were admitted to become rich firstly and the government wish them can lead the other majorities to become rich together. It's easier said than done. We love wealth but we need get them in a proper way. We respect those who get richer through hard work and honesty.

But unfortunately, the cruel reality is that many of these few people don't want to share the wealth fruit with other Chinese people. They pay low salary to their employees and deliver their big wealth abroad. They collude with some greedy officials for bigger illegal earnings. Greediness of human nature causes more and more corruption in the world and when the law-executors and public power get involved in this, the bad situation seems to be with no end.

Challenge No. 2: Unfair distribution of income intensifies conflicts.

For those who became rich firstly, they can use the present money to earn more and more money for the game rule stands on their side. But those who now is poor must work for those riches and there is a long-term process for them to get rich from rags. In the ancient time, there was an Imperial

Examination nationwide in China. I think its positive

side is that there always existed a passageway for the lower-level people to enter the higher-level of the society. Maybe it is behind the times, but it's a truth that no matter who get the control of a nation, they must give everyone hope and fairness in the game rule can benefit both sides.

Nowadays in China, the game rule is set by the vested interests group including the governors and those swift-footed minority riches. They held their gainings so tightly that smaller and smaller space is left for the late-comers. About the wealth and fortune, we don't have a structured value system to propagate fairness and kindness. I think two peaceful ways can balance the unfairness of the income distribution.

Way No. 1: Higher-rate tax to the riches. For the rich more rich and poor more poor situation get worse and worse. To avoid the violent revolution that compulsively distribute the resource which causes blood / death and disaster, tax tool is a life-saving straw for the China rulers. Of course another powerful solution on fighting against corruption is absolutely necessary.

Way No. 2: Innovation on every field of the society. We need break when we feel closed and isolated. Any kinds of corruption and dishonesty mainly are caused by stasis of developing and unchanging ideology. If the world is active with innovation and new things, it produce more opportunities and offer more chances and ways to make fortune, which also bring fairness and justice naturally but not artificially. Of course basis for this way need more factors and I think the most important two are education and the quality level of the citizens. Human quality is the basis of any basises, whether on thoughts or behaviors.

Chinese was not a folk of innovation yesterday, but changes may happen tomorrow in this fun and colorful Global Village.

Challenge No. 3: Clash between the people and grass-roots governors

There ever existed many dynasties in China's long history. Their establishments and perishments over and over again proved it an unchanged natural law that the people is the water which can

Some grass-roots governors

carry the boat as well as overturn it.

China is the biggest developing country in the world. The only thing unchanged is that everything is changing anytime. The benefit distribution is rebuild and reconstructed on many fields and for all these reconstructions are based on a very backward situation. Old life style are transformed and new changes are breaking the old order of the country. The changes get different influence on different people or groups and this caused different clashes between the people and the governments.

As the frontline to the public, the grass-roots governors are facing a plenty of specific problems on dealing with the new contradictions and executing the new policies. I think the way to solve these is that the grass-roots governors need pay enough patience and put needs of the people in the center of everything, and basis for this is that the governors must personally experience the real hardship of the common people, but not just stay at the form or surface.

Challenge No. 4: The contradiction between excessive-priced housing and people's low income

Housing price has been a headachy issue in China

for more than 10 years' time. Reasons as following mainly caused the higher price:

First, as peoples' living conditions improves, the demand of housing increased rapidly.

Second, more and more people move to cities from their home in rural country and the population grows.

Third, the cost of material / labor rise rapidly.

Fourth, speculators in real estate market push the price higher.

Fifth, Land sales is the main source of the local governments' finance and its higher price to the real estate agents finally will become part of the housing price and transfer to the common consumers.

China is a nation with the biggest population in the world. This biggest base data  makes the average income of individuals still lower but the needs for housing increase more rapidly. Then the contradiction occurs. For several times Chinese government attempted to improve this by macro-control but effects are small even aggravated the worse market. So there have many disputes about this. Some think macro-control need be continuous but others think market get self-cure function and macro-control made things worse. I think the way for solving is that government just act as its public role and build more low-rent houses and guarantee houses for those immigrants and common citizens.

Challenge No. 5: The crisis of integrity

Integrity means good faith, which is the soul of a harmonious society. Sometimes when we go after fortune, we may lose the good faith. The bad faith is an evil animal, it will swallow ourselves' and others' conscience. Timely propaganda of good faith is the lube oil of the human kindness.

Challenge No. 6: Democratic political reform effects is below the public expection

This is a great world now we are living. Internet and high-tech make nothing is impossible. Transparency of information is the catalyzer of democracy. Freedom of speech is undoubtedly a common view in this great age. Relax and communication are much more welcomed than suppression and isolation. This makes everyone more and more equal in status and confluent in thoughts. The real democracy prevailing can't be held back.

But the benefits of different groups especially benefits of the vested interests groups make it easy to be said but hard to de done for the democracy. Then in China just a clean-handed and clearheaded government can be up to the demands for higher-level democratic environment. Then the only way for the government is to faithfully go deep to the masses. Standing high above the masses can only lead to take basis away from yourself.

Challenge No. 7:　Pollution and ecocrisis

Any kind of gain gets a loss of another kind. We are enjoying the happiness and convenience of modern life. Various products and goods were made here and there and were transported from here to there. Then pollution and kinds of rubbish became another form of

substance around us. Sand storm / water resource pollution / haze in big cities etc. get usual in our surrounding. The

17

objective world challenges human with more and more problems.

But less people in China care more about this crisis. Most of Chinese think the bad results are far away from them and they seldom consider that this may hurt our descendants. I think potent propaganda in public about this can gradually set up the concept of environment protection among the masses and related laws must be established and enforced.

Challenge No. 8: Aged tendency of the population

Human have invented so many high-tech in medical field on anti aging and prolonging life. This directly lead to a result 10 or 20 years later that the aged group will become a bigger part of the society. That will be a big burden for the society and the younger of each family must take much more responsibility to take care of the older parents and grandparents. Although the productive efficiency highered and can maintain people's living condition, there still will appear more new situations and challenges which we now can't properly predict . At least we must establish a perfect endowment insurance and medical security system.

Challenge No. 9: Awkwardness of the employment of College graduates

During the past 20-30 years, because of the poor basis of China and there were so many blank fields and positions needed to develop and this made abundant demands of college graduates. There was ever a time that entering college was a main road for destiny changing especially for those low-level crowd.

But things changes as time goes by. After 30 yeas' developing, The whole wealth was accumulated and different benefit clusters were formed and the society game rule was also changed. The college entrance examination is no more as powerful as before and the college graduates' fate more and more depends on their family or gregarious background. One with poor background must devote much more than ever to overstep the barriers caused by  the new fortune distributing situation.

Although the situation is awkward but it's not hopeless. Although a college graduate might be jobless, his or her parents are still on two positions of the society. I think this is fair for them because there automatically will limit the distributed resource of every unit of the families. and we can predict that within some certain period in the future there will occur a shortage of labor force because of the stream of retirement of their parents. The birth planning policy will get an effect of one taking occupation of 2 or 4 jobs in the future which will cause multiple skills demands for the individuals and there maybe many low-level jobs facing shortage of employees and higher price will be quoted for these posts and again manual workers will be higher paid than the mental workers .

Challenge No. 10: Values and trend of thoughts will become multifarious and space of main values will be compressed.

As the world get smaller and smaller in our mind and internet is everywhere, brainstorms also get usual and normal. Maybe one will change his values or ideologies in his or her life several times for different experiences in the colorful world. Main values nowadays might lose some market or space and the related changes may get related effects. These are also the results of the advocation of fairness and freedom.

Author's points

People in the world get more and more integrated. One affects one another closely and challenges to the human being must be recognized by everyone. If these were aware of by everyone, we can make this world a better one.

In many fields of China, it seems to meet the blind alley. People can't see the clear future and get confused. The government says everyday to adjust the economic structure and encourage innovation. But they don't know how to achieve that practically for they stayed in the office for a long time and lost the feelings of the real market and reality. Then they think taking example of other developed countries' experience is the right way. But simply grafting doesn't adapt to China's specialties. Then we must do a lot of research and practice to set up and stabilize a new construction of the nation.

3. About " Made in China "

Nowadays, " Made in China" is widely known by the world. During the past 20 years, " Made in China" is a name card of China and gradually rest of the world began to know a new China which is no more just tea / silk / ancient palace / hair braid. The world depends more and more on " Made in China", which brought up the fact and miracle that China is now the second largest economical entity of the world and the first largest country in manufacturing industry output value.

Lower cost / cheaper labor / higher energy consumption / higher overdraft of environment / pollution / price dumping / international trading dispute...... We get so many keywords about " Made in China " that it's hard to conclude whether it's good or bad for " Made in China ".

Challenged by China and for the reason of the domestic higher jobless rate, America has a plan to withdraw its investments from China, which force

China to adjust its economic structure and promote the innovation. According to the insiders' research, China get full equipped industrial chain on high end / middle end / low end area. China's speedy development in the past three decades depended much on the undertaking of transferred industry on middle end and low end from the developed regions. More devotion on high end manufacturing area will be the key to get more share in the global competition.

It need to discuss whether China's enormous manufacturing industry can be continuous or not. Land / raw materials and lower-cost labor ever supported China's development. But price and cost of these all raised for the available resource get more and more scarce. Gradually China is losing its previous advantages.

Most of the " Made in China " are in form of OEM. There still has a long way to go for Chinese enterprises to established their own famous brands which demand much more on hardware and software.

Hereby we make more deep analysis about " Made in China ".

3-1. Degree of recognition about " Made in China " abroad.

A. In America

American is a folk care more about innovation. If one get an idea, it is easer for him or her to get an investment and make the dream come true in the market. People like new and creative things in America.

But in China, although people say about innovation everyday, there still have less chance for those ones with new ideas because China doesn't have a system of encouraging and investing on the innovation. the old system is still strong and influence the whole country much. Somewhat culture from China's 5000 years' history is a burden for China's

development because it hinder the freedom of people's thoughts. Then less innovation make China's manufacturing industry still remain on the point of imitating and copying the outdated achievements of other countries.

The consumers from America are nit-pick. Their demands are various and high-rate. That's why products from China can't reach higher price although their quality is OK. Shortage of innovation and lack of intellectual property might be the main reasons.

USA president Obama is now carrying out the revive of " Made in USA" to strengthen American

economical basis then to avoid the high risk of high bubble from the high-proportioned financial economy. I think this is the correct path for it can compact the structure of the nation's economy then there has a new strong arm to protect people's welfare and cut down the high rate of joblessness, which is also a bad news for China and other developing countries whose economy is mainly formed from OEM or other styles of intermediary business.

B. In Asia

Comparing with America, people in Asia are less educated and for this reason their needs are lower-rate. Then good-quality and cheap products made in China become their favorites. Certainly these countries don't include Japan and South Korea.

C. In Africa

Without doubt, Africa is the most successful land for China's strategy. " Made in China" is more welcomed here than anywhere else. Not only real products are popular here, but also Chinese films and movies are highly praised here. To a certain extent, the experience of China's development is a mirror for these Africa countries.

3-2. Problems and disadvantages of " Made in China "

As " Made in China " expanding overseas step by step, there occur different opinions about it. Some said " Made in China" will reappear the brilliance of "

Made in America " and " Made in Japan ". In fact, when " Made in China " get more and more share of the international market, problems of it also accumulated as follow:

Problem No. 1: There have no famous brands

Brand effect is infinitely great. When your brand has been around and people get a habit to buy your brand, profits can be produced by themselves.

According to the latest data, " Made in China " in the fields of energy / chemical / building materials / textile / household appliances / electron have reached to the biggest output in the world. But it's funny that in the top 100 famous brands of the world, brands from America / Japan and German take up 2/3 of them and there is nearly blank for the Chinese brands. It means that most of the products made in China have just been pasted others' logo and most of the earnings have been split by the terminal brand holders and dealers.

This is unfair for China, especially for those Chinese industrial workers who spent more than 12 hours everyday on the assembly lines. But reality is cruel and Reasons for this is that China lost the first chance of international marketing and have to be led

by nose. Ignorance on Brands building and shortage of innovation on technology researching and marketing make " Made in China " on a passive status and there are no possibilities to get higher profits and just stay at the end of the production chain.

Problem No. 2: Major equipments depend on importing

As we mentioned above, China just earns the lowest profits by simple fabrication. For a matured economy entity, it's a key mark for it to have independent manufacturing machine tools. But in China, most of the precision machines and major equipments depend on importing from other developed countries. In a global industrial system, machine tools manufacturers is on the top of the value chain and the downstream enterprises can just be the workshops of the upstream firms. Then any moves or troubles of the upstream firms will influence the fate of those weak downstream enterprises. We give an example of Chinese Auto industry, Almost all the electronic components are imported from abroad and many China Auto firms just settle for assembling parts into one, which gets less technology contents and of course get no brand effects.

Then whether we can make advanced machine tools or not determines whether or not we can get an independent and integrated industrial system, which can bring stable and continuous profits and developments.

Problem No. 3: Pretty low profit

Profit is an important indicator for measuring if an enterprise or a country is matured or strong one. Profits in manufacturing industry mainly come from brand value / core technology / intellectual property / designing / high-tech components and material flow etc. The most obvious character of " Made in China " is processing of materials supplied by clients, which doesn't get the core technology and intellectual property then causes lower add value and profit rate. Without the basis of profits, China can just be a big manufacturing country but not a strong one and it's impossible to proceed the further innovation or break.

29

This may become a vicious circle if the problem of profit can't be solved.

Problem No. 4: Neglection about intellectual property and lack of industrial standards

During these present 10 years, anti-dumping investigation / technical barrier / intellectual property litigation get more and more usual on " Made in China ". Carelessness of intellectual property and industrial standards cause great limitation for China's manufacturing industry.

In the earlier years of " Made in China", carelessness of intellectual property and industrial standards brought higher efficiency of China's economic development. But as time goes by, higher and higher demands in the international market challenge " Made in China ".

In certain ways, standards mean order and measure of the industry and economy. Our world is changing so fast that more and more new things appear and there need more and more standards to standardize them. In the future, who get the standards will get the power of the world.

3-3. Advantages of " Made in China "

Of course, " Made in China " gets its advantages making it well-known and hot sold in the global market.

A. Lower labor cost

China's large population is the endless source for the labor market . The unbalanced economy level of agriculture and industry and the regional difference determine that the lower labor cost will still last for 10-20 years.

B. Higher quality of the labor force

Compulsory and high-grade education get more and more popular in China. This make the labor force can meet the updating needs of the future situation.

C. Great potential of the domestic market

Huge market means great potential from all kinds of fields. When the overseas market get fatigued and weak, China's big domestic market is always an anti-risk basis and will digest most of the production of " Made in China ".

D.   Peaceful society and stable political environment

After 30 years of speedy developing, China get an adequate foreign currency reserves and the exchange rate is stable. This offer a safe and reliable environment for those foreign investments.

Author's points

Creation on technology is the key factor to promote the overall quality and updating of " Made in China ". China can no longer just be the assembler and need to devote more in integrating and creating.

The Chinese people is not a folk good at creating and innovation. The main content of its culture serve the needs of rulers and people here get used to obeying and being ruled. It's now modern age and changes are world-shaking. Sometimes we are confused of how to make the choice before the complicated things. Maybe simple and peaceful life is the best one for us to choose.

4. Outline of China's history

Not to spend much time on the details of China's history, I hereby choose the main chapters and sections as the outline.

4-1. Prehistoric age

As early as 1.7 million year ago, There has been human trace on China land. About 700-200 thousand  years ago, the Beijing ape began to use fire and for the first time human being got an ability of control the nature. Nearly 18000 years ago, the Beijing Upper Cave Man who had already had obvious character of yellow race not only can make fire artificially, but also invented the first bone needle for sewing. About 6-7 thousand years ago, in Yellow River basin there appeared culture of colored pottery and black pottery. In Yangtze River basin, people can use big wood to construct buildings.

Nearly 4 thousand years ago, Emperor of Huang

won the final success in the tribal war. He was respected as the " The first humanity originator " by the later generations. Afterwards there appeared several outstanding people: Yao / Sun and Yu.

4-2. Xia / Shang / Zhou Dynasty

Xia Dynasty was founded in 2100 B.C by Yu . His son Qi inherited the throne and started the hereditary system in China. Xia was the earliest slave-owner's state in China and lasted 471 years with 17 kings.

In 1600 B.C, King of Tang of Shang Tribe ended Xia's ruling and established Shang Dynasty. In 1400 B.C, Shang moved its capital to Yin and then Shang Dynasty get another name - Yin Dynasty.  Shang is the main developing period of slave-owner system of China. Shang lasted 554 years with 17 generations and 31 kings.

Zou was the last king of Shang and he was nasty

and cruel. In 1100 B.C, King of Wu of Zhou Tribe led his army overthrew Shang and set up Zhou Dynasty. In the history, Zhou was divided into West Zhou and East Zhou. In West Zhou period time of King of Li, the citizens and slaves revolted and in 771 B.C the Minority Dirong People scored Capital Gaojing and killed Zhou's king You, then West Zhou perished. You's son King of Ping moved the capital to Luoyi and established East Zhou, which including Spring and Autumn period and Warring states age.

4-3. Spring and Autumn period / Warring states age

From 770 B.C to 476 B.C was the Spring and Autumn Period of China. Slave-owner's system began to collapse. Central power of Zhou was weaken and the vassal states raised up for competition of land and sphere of influence.

From 475 B.C to 221 B.C was the Warring States Age of China. The feudalism came into being. There finally appear seven main kingdoms Qi / Chu / Yan / Zhao / Han / Wei / Qin and they fought year after year for the power of the nation.

4-4. Qin unified the whole nation into

one.

After a series of domestic reforms, Qin became the most powerful kingdom in China . It defeated the other six and unified the whole nation again in 220 B.C. Qin named itself the Qin empire and it was the first unitive and centralized feudalism country in China's history. Qin started the the system of prefectures and counties, unified the currency / written language / weights and measures, built roads and the Great wall. But Qin Dynasty lasted shortly and its cruel ruling caused its perishment.

4-5. The period of two Han dynasties

In 202 B.C, after defeated Xiangyu, Liu Bang

established Han Dynasty and located the capital at Changan, known to history as " West Han". At the beginning of Han, the rulers learned the lesson from Qin's perishing and carry out the policy of rehabilitating, lessening the exploitation and tax from people. There ever had extremely powerful and prosperous situation in China.

In 8 B.C, Wang mang usurp state power and Changed the title of dynasty into Xin. This caused the nationwide rebellion. In the year of 25, Han's imperial clansman Liu xiu got the success and restored the Han dynasty, known to history as " East Han". Liu xiu ruled the nation by means of " Mild and flexible", strenthening the central power and lessening the farmers' burden. After years' effort, the society became stable and economic is prosperous.

4-6. Three Kingdoms period and Two Jin Dynasties / Northern and Southern Dynasties

During the end years of East Han, there had storm and stress on the China land. Warlords fought one another. Till the year of 208, Cao cao's son Cao pi / Liu bei / Sun quan respectively established their kingdoms Wei / Shu and Wu, and being tripartite balance of forces of the country.

In 263, Wei extinguished Shu, Two years later Sima yan launched a palace coup and established Jin dynasty (" West Jin "). In 280, Jin extinguished Wu and reunified China. In 291, internal disorder occurred in West Jin and " War of the eight princes " began and soon West Jin died out. In 317, Sima rui set the capital at Jianye in South China. But in north China, The nomadic tribes one after another established their regimes and there ever had sixteen kingdoms in the north China. In 439,  North Wei unified the north China into one and soon divided into West Wei and East Wei. Later East wei was replaced by North Qi and West Wei was usurped by North Zhou. Now we call West Wei / East Wei / West Wei / North Qi / North Zhou as " Northern Dynasties ". In south China there ever had Qi / Song / Liang / Chen four dynasties and now we call them as " Southern Dynasties "

4-7. Sui and Tang Dynasties

In 581, Great officer Yang jian dethroned the emperor and established his Sui dynasty. In 589, he conquered Chen and made a new unite of China. It announced the end of divided situation of the land. In 600, Yang guang succeeded to the throne. But this is an extremely extravagant and luxurious one, and people again went back to the suffering days. Later Yu wenhua killed Yang guang and Sui dynasty ended. Warlord of Tang Li yuan unified the nation by war and established Tang Dynasty. In 626, his son Li shiming launched the famous " Xuanwu Gate Coup ", killed his two brothers and became the emperor. When he was on the throne, there appeared the golden years of China, and China was the biggest and the most prosperous country in the world. In 690, Li shiming's daughter-in-law Wu zetian dethroned her husband and made herself the first female emperor of China, Changed the nation title into " Zhou ". But in 705, her son restored and Changed the  nation title back to " Tang ". In 712, Li longji inherited the crown and emphasized on state managing. In the earlier years of his reign, China again appeared strong and prosperous. But Later Li longji misused traitor ministers and then there occurred " AnShi Disturbances ". Since then Tang's power got more and more weak and In 907 Huang cao ended Tang. China's history entered into a new page.

4-8. Five Dynasties and Ten Kingdoms / Liao / Xia / Two Song Dynasties

Since Zhu wen set up Liang Dynasty in 907, early or late there appeared Tang / Jin / Han / Zhou dynasties in the central area of China and ten locality separatist power in south and north China, Which was known to history as " Five Dynasties and Ten Kingdoms Period ".

In 960, a military mutiny happened at Chenqiao county by Zhao Kuangyin and then he established Song dynasty by replacing North Zhou. Cenral China again was reunified into one. During this period, The Qidan Folk established Liao dynasty in the north China. In 1038, Li yuanhao established Xia dynasty in northwest China. In 1115, The Nvzhen Folk established Big Jin Dynasty.

In 1127, Big Jin's troop captured Song's capital and two of Song's emperors Hui and Qin were put in prison. North Song Dynasty ended and remnants of Song withdrew to south China known to history as " South Song ".

4-9. Yuan / Ming / Qing Dynasties

In 1206, Genghis Khan unified the tribes of Mongolia and after years of war he destoryed Jin and Xia, the north China became one. In 1271, Hubilie established Yuan dynasty and conquered South Song in 1297. Yuan was a country with broad territory.

During the end years of Yuan, the social contradictions became acute and people rose up everywhere. In 1368, Zhu yuanzhang enthroned at Yingtian and established Ming dynasty. After he died, Zhu di launched the " Jinnan Rebellion " and seized

the crown. In 1421, he moved the capital to Beijing.

In the later period of Ming, the rulers were decadent and corrupt. This caused the people's uprising. In 1644, Li zicheng established Shun regime in Xian and soon captured Beijing, Ming died out.

Nuerhaci, the leader of Nvzhen Folk upstarted in northeast China and established Late Jin regime in 1616. In 1636, Huang taiji changed the title of Late Jin to Qing and began the Qing dynasty. In 1644, Qing troop entered the central China and defeated Li zicheng. China was under the control of Qing.

Qing experienced a prosperous period from Kangxi to Qianlong Age. But since Daoguang Age, China's national power got weak and then in 1840 China's gate was broken by foreign forces.

4-10. Modern history of China

Since 1840, China became a semi-colonial and semi-feudal society. In 1851, the Taiping Rebellion led by Hong xiuquan damaged Qing's domination. In 1911, the Xinhai Revolution broke out and Qing Collapsed. It's the final end of China's 2000 years' feudalism.

In 1919, the " May fourth Movement " broke out in China and it's a milestone of China's new-democratic revolution. In 1924, The communist party and Kuomintang carried out the first cooperation and defeated the Northern warlords. In 1927, Jiang jieshi, leader of Kuomintang ended the cooperation. The communist party began to set up its own army and revolutionary base area. In 1937, These two began the second round of cooperation to fight against Japanese invader. After 8 years' hard fighting, Japan surrendered

in 1945. In 1949, after defeated Kuomintang, the communist party established the People's Republic Of China.

Author's points

It's a brief of China's history and I wish this can show you a frame of China's past. Maybe it's not very useful, but it can help you better understand China.

About history, it's not only the simple cases and events, but also records that lead us to think and follow its positive factors to build and live in our present world.

5. About Chinese culture

There have many definitions about culture and they defined culture from different angles, but it's a hard job to do this and so far no one can give culture a perfect and accepted wording. Generally speaking, culture is a social phenomenon and a result caused by long term of human evolution. Culture is unseen and different culture get different effect on different people in different period.

Properly speaking, in those days when science and technology was backward and traffic was inaccessible, culture was more related to a certain folk or country limited in certain region. it includes history / geography / tradition / custom / life style / literature / art / code of conduct / thinking mode / values and so on.

5-1. Confucianism

Chinese traditional culture is long-standing / well-established / broad and profound. Confucian culture was the main stream and key part of Chinese traditional culture, which was hold in esteem by the governing class and intellectuals.

Nearly 2500 years ago, Confucius started Confucianism. It was not created without foundation and most of its theory were on the basis of introspection / serious analysis and revise about the past cultural heritage after the great social turmoil.

Mercy and righteousness are the core of  Confucianism. One need to self-cultivate the virtue / moral and be harmonious with the surroundings. Mercy and righteousness is of all things and even one should give up his or her life to achieve the values of mercy and righteousness.

" A jade without carving will not become a useful jade, a man without education will not know the righteousness. " it's a famous saying from Confucianism and it advocates that education plays an important role in social development. The education is not just for the fewer people from uppertendom but for all the people without discrimination.

5-2. Taoism

Taoism, a main genre of ancient China's thoughts. Its core idea are Tao / nothing / nature and instinct.

Taoism thinks that Tao is the original source of everything of the world, and everything changes according to their respective nature and instinct. The big Tao also changes in accordance with regulations.

Inactivity is another main opinion of Taoism. Since everything gets their nature and regulation, there is no need to change things artificially and the right way is to let them be naturally as they are.

5-3. Buddhism

Buddhism was come from ancient India and it spread to China in West Han Period. Combined with Chinese local Confucianism, it got its special characters in China. It advocates that one need insist  on kindness and stop doing bad.

It also emphasizes self-cultivating and teaches people to deeply believe in cause and effect, and help others and self-helping to achieve the best result or effect.

After more than 1000 years' fusion and till Song dynasty, there had been a combination of the Confucianism / Taoism and Buddhism. They influence Chinese people from generation to generation.

For self-cultivating, Confucianism praises highly about respecting, Taoism advocates silence and Buddhism emphasizes cleanness in soul.

Author's points

Culture is a complicated and mixed accumulation of every thing. Our social life has three main basic area: economy / politics / culture. Economy is the basis, politics is the concentrated expression of economy and culture is the reflection of the former two.

In the culture exchanging, we must treat every kind of culture equally and get along in harmory.

6. Residuary from trouble days

22nd, August, 2013, a day may be common for most of the common Chinese people who were busy for livelihood but never common for those who we call them " Public servants ". Bo xilai, ever a top official with influence in China, but now notorious for his corruption / abuse of power and bribe-taking. it's the day for him to be sentenced by the court.

Before his disclosure, Bo was ever at the top of power in Chongqing, a major central-controlled city of China. At the beginning of his term of office, he carried out a suppression on evil forces in the whole city and the structure of power in Chongqing was rebuilt. But during the process of rebuilding the authority order, he was extremely self-centered and everything was decided by his say. Others can't share his spotlight and Bo also carry out the cult of personality, wanted to set up his great personal charisma and image among the masses. but any voice opposing him would be suppressed and even arrested. In a way, he is a dictator.

People born in 1950's and even earlier all experienced those trouble days 50 years ago - The Culture Revolution. That was a period that human nature and individuality were severely oppressed. The China land was full of criticism and struggle. One could attack others by big character poster, everything was concerned with politics and people dare not to speak and any words in mistake may cause a big misfortune to him or her even their families. Red storm carried everything with one.

During those days, there were no laws and public

security organs. Maoism was the only law and everyone should obey it with no excuse. Conflict and struggle were artificially created among the masses, which were divided into several different classes. Those who obey Maoism were revolutionaries, and those who got different opinions were anti-revolutionaries and would be destoryed. People didn't have choices for living or dying and all the country was under the atmosphere of Red Terror. People didn't get the rights of controlling their own time and they have to spend most of their time to have meetings and shout slogans. They had no rights to create and occupy properties. They had no rights to get education and were forced to learn Maoism and political thoughts. The pupils overthrew the teachers and the normal education was damaged.

Nowadays, these phenomenon again get a trend to reappear in China. Bo xilai is a typical case. He carried out left-leaning policies and thoughts in Chongqing, which cause negative effects on local economy and many enterprises had to move to other places because of the reduction of investing environment. There began to appear space for the residuary of those trouble days. Of course we can understand that it get its reasons. Many people got weak and poor in the process of the distribution of social fortune for the unfair rules which was ignored in the high-speed development of economy. Then a great deal of people cherish the memory of the equalitarianism in that period. Now we are living in a times full of all kinds of competition. Many people get failed in the competition and then they wish equalitarianism can solve their problems caused by their awkward situation.

We surely need fairness and equality because they are two key factors in a better and stable society and can never be neglected. We respect the facts and strongly oppose the extremism. Any form of extreme leftism or rightism are both bad for the world. There always need a balance in our society and everyone's mind. We advocate the  fairness and equality after everyone's relevant hard work. The lessons from the trouble days is that people wanted to use violent force to equally divide the social properties but not by creating through labor.

Author's points

We can not extremely wholly deny a thing. Sometimes when we oppose something, in fact more or less we also get effected by it and it may cause another wrong extreme. China has a long history of advocating centrism and this is proved to be wise and correct. But when we put this into effect, balancing is the key and we need to make adjustments when things get dangerously extreme. Of course the basis of the adjustments must be the main needs of most of the people and the fairness and equality. Nowadays, facing more and more complicated social problems, an abundantly experienced and strongly responsible government must emphasize their efforts on reducing the popular discontent and pushing proper policies to produce more and more opportunities to activate the circulation of the social fortune. If there is a fair and efficient social system for marketing and distribution, everyone will get equal chances and make their colorful dreams come true.

7. Experience from developed countries

Developing is the main topic of our period especially for China. Taking example by the historical experience can give us many revelations, especially from the experience of the developed countries.

From the meaning of modernization, China is still an country backward in many fields especially in the education of the citizens. We can not limit our eyes just on the cities, 800 million of farmers in the suburban area occupy the big share of China's population.

7-1. About education

The quality of the citizens of a country mostly depends on this country's education level. Never neglect the quality of the citizens, barycenter of the society is determined by this and it will reconstruct the world on certain time point in the future.

People first is one of the topic of the present world. But I don't think this runs well in China. On most occasion, people care more about the needs of themselves'. Then we can not say it's people first but self first. That's why China facing more and more social problems and difficulties. If the whole world's value system doesn't keep the step of economic development, order of the world may meet great challenge from negative sides. The two main issues are corruption and unequal distribution of income.

Then education is the key to build the value system. This is confirmed by history and other developed countries' experience. Value system is something to do with ideology and things in people's mind. Who controls people's mind controls the whole world. 50 years ago the revolution of culture in China was an obvious and strong example, although it's not good, it's really an evidence for the power of extreme ideology and education.

What do we want to do and where do we want to go determines how should we educate and be educated. This is the mankind's kingly way. Sometimes we care more about ourselves but less about the others. this is the reason why our world still exists unfairness and many kinds of problems. We can not perish these but we can limit these as much as possible. More fair is everyone to the others, more harmonious our world will be.

7-2. About innovation

When a thing occurs in the world, it may experience the beginning, developing and declining. When it declining, it faces bottleneck problems. This is an unchanged regulation for everything. To slow down this, we need ideas and actions of innovation.

Chinese is a folk not good at innovation mostly because of its conservative culture background, which causes that the whole country always is in an atmosphere of shortage of vitality. I think the way to solve this is to encourage people to release their potential and change their mind from those old-fashioned things to a completely new mode. We should build an environment of any kinds of innovation and then there will be full of vigour and opportunities in our society.

In the developed countries, there has a long history of marketing economy and sufficient competition forced people to innovate otherwise they will lose the game. It's a natural rule in the marketing world and the market can determine and control everything. Surely market also get its weakness and so there need a lot of laws and rules to standardize and limit the market and people's behaviors.

7-3. About competition

In China we still need to advocate competition, but no more in low level such as price war or inter-companies attacking, which causes loss at both sides. High-leveled competition need high-quality persons and anti-unfair competition laws also is a must. Competition out of order may lead to the waste of natural resources and hurt the social morality. Good faith and fairness should be emphasized in everyone's mind and then we can make our world running in a proper way.

7-4. About anti-corruption

American has the most honest government in the

world. It has a complete budget system with strong execution. Complete marketing economy makes it gets self-cure functions. All these make corruption seldom happens in America.

China has a long history of centralism and this makes resource distribution bind with power and authority, which gets a great deal of space for corruption. Especially this system influenced people's thoughts for thousands of years and it's deep-rooted in Chinese people's mind. Then anti-corruption is really a hard and difficult task that has a long way to go. It is related to many factors such as citizen education and system reform. But the final goal we pursue is to build a public awareness atmosphere about anti-corruption.

Author's points

China is an ancient nation with a long history. Culture heritages are abundant and influence every corner of the country. The main character of this kind of culture is traditional and conservative. People's intelligence are less discovered and people here get used to observe rules and regulations with great servility. To a certain extent, Chinese people are not suitable for marketing economy and Changing people's mind is really a hard job. But as the globlization steps, values of Freedom and innovation spread all over the world. Let's pray for the better future.

8. People's mind determines the world

We have never met a time point like nowadays. But we have to admit it's really a golden age more advanced than any time ever before. We see things completely different new and our eyeballs ever get tired of these. We ever get lost and confused because we ever wanted more for our greediness. Success is rare, which is not for everybody at least in the sense of the common meaning of the success if it concerning money or power.

One's mind is full of thoughts and images. The strength of thoughts and images are determined by the frequency and depth that they were taken effect accordingly. In the past three decades, China experienced gradual processes of opening and releasing in different fields. The elder generations might be backward in thoughts and ideas then we can not change things completely in a short time for we must take account of the feelings of the elders. Any kind of thought movements can't avoid pains or changeless idles, and it surely will take a long time, Especially in China with a long history and conservative custom.

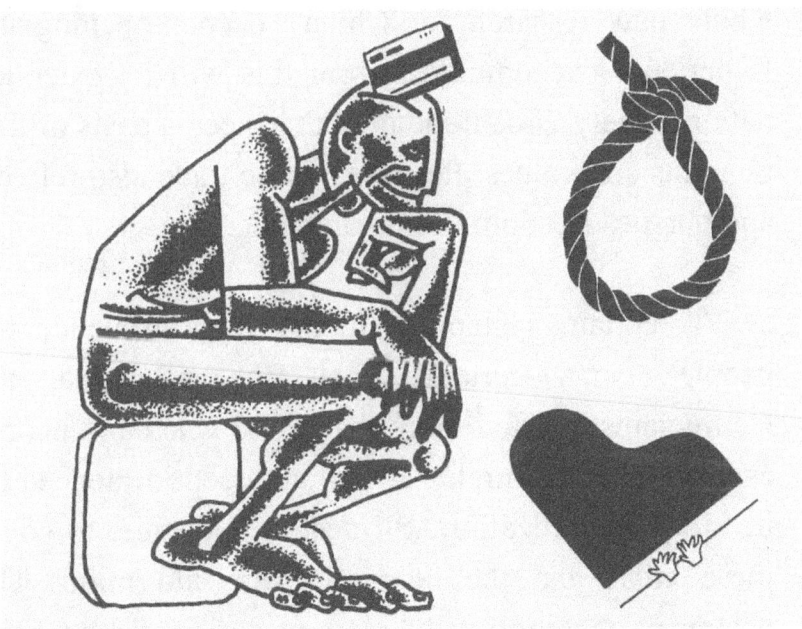

Youth is the future and they grow up together with so many fancy things which are unimaginable for the earlier generations that we will face a magic and hopeful world in the future. But for the different understanding or ideas about things by different generations, conflicts, contradictions and discriminations will exist and also may lead to some negative or positive effects. No matter what they will be, we always wish we can live in a peaceful world.

September 29th, 2013 may be a day getting special meaning in the history of China's opening up. Shanghai Free Trade Zone was unveiled. This is a whole new research for China's deeper opening up. Experiences accumulated from this will be extended nation-widely. Free trade of course need a basis of free thoughts and values. Purpose of free trade also reflects and pursues freedom of human being.

A certain system of theory may influence the people for a certain time. But in China, the Confucianism lasted more than 2000 years and people especially in the rural area still are deep influenced by it. Modern civilization still need a long time to cover these areas and the people's heart and mind. The backward condition is the main reason for this and this also means a great potential market for the morden things. If the people learn to consume the new things, big fortune behind this can cause a lot of opportunities. People's mind can be changed by heavily inspiring new things and ideas and this causes people's new lifestyle, and then new chances / new fortune and new order appear.

I still remember the days in the school. Our soul was impressed by those stiff theories such as sticking to the socialism / the leadership of   communist party / the dictatorship of the people and the opening up. Till now, things and world changed so much, these things may be no more impressive in our mind and we can just call these ideals or utopia. Our minds have been performed operations by life , The reality is cruel and it's easy for one to lose his or her beliefs.

Author's points

This might be a little optimistic. We have to admit the remnant and inertance of old system are so strong and it need time for the new trend. I think for this we need to call on those social elites to be more responsible to pay more devotion on good faith and fairness. Of course things will be hard and difficult if these strong figures or groups get no idea to transfer or share their resources or fortunes to the public. That's why I emphasize many times that an health and efficient social environment should be a result that everyone participates and devotes. Never forget that a small smile and a hand to the weak can make our world more beautiful.

9. True economy situation in China

Marketing economy in China gets a prefix--**Getting China's features**. It's just a saying but can hide many things. I'd say that China's economy gets marketing characters only in the coastal cities but

in most areas of its territory there still remain the strong shadow of planning character. We give it a name Official-business economy. Officials still play a key role in the economy, which is a continuation of the old centralism system. The business men don't spend more time on their business but much more on engaging to set up relationship to official departments. They invite officials to have dinner and some details are related to corruption. In the inland area of China planning economy actually runs obviously. If you want to start a business you need cross many steps and take a long time to get the certification from the government and power of government is still considered as the force to determine everything.

This situation must be changed, at least the powerful governmental authority need to be weaken to shorten the gap between top-status public power and a common citizen, then it can make things more equal and fair. In most of time power is the breeding ground of corruption and evil. What we need to is to make the government more trustworthy and credible but not more power-centered or isolated. The officials need to get rid of those fogyish ideas from their brains and be more open-minded, especially they need to experience and practice in the real market. People admire officials who get real skills and rich experience in marketing but not in planning with no investigations.

Certainly, all these need a key basis. That is the people's awareness. If the people want to control themselves' fate, then deepen the marketing economy and people can make their own choices more freely. If the people want to be lazy and be arranged, then continue the governmental planning. Maybe this is a proposition meaningless for any attempt to guess people's desire is one-sided and unbalanced. Then Marketing economy is better for it give people more freedom and regulation of marketing can adjust and balance things automatically. But it need time in China, at least another new generation with new ideas and values become the main stream of the country.

Author's points

This doesn't sentence the end of planning economy. when the marketing competition gets disorderly and people suffer from this more, I think governmental planning will still play a strong role. The world not just contains marketing and planning. Man's fate is as uncertain as the weather and the moon will wax and wane. There is no final conclusion for this and we wish the world can become better and better.

10. Consuming engine need to restart

Consuming is the footstone of marketing economy. As the main body of consuming, consumers' confidence / mentality and behavior determine all things. Pay attention that these three come in a sequential order-- Confidence to mentality and then finally behavior.

I can't remember the actual time when I get to know the word of "Market", At least not in my childhood. In those days things we ate or we used were

    all arranged and got a upper limit of quota. Planning was prevalent on a large scale. This lasted till I was in my teenage and my rice quota was 21.5kg every month. Few people got concept of market and then there was no market for anything but anything had a huge potential for market. Since the middle of 1980's, Consuming of real subjects began and

gradually increased. From bike to TV to icebox to air conditioner..............then to cars and housing, we experienced the process from poor days to rich life and this can be called the first round of domestic consuming. Nowadays there is no problem to survive for the basic living condition and the substance and meaning of consuming are no more the traditional definitions or descriptions in books or people's mind.

In the past 10 years, Consuming in China was sluggish and common people dared not consume boldly and confidently. Reason for this is that no one could give a certain promise about a stable future to calm down the people's worries. The Chinese people get a character of not daring to meet risks. They like stable life and any kind of risk may be considered to be dangerous. This is why we often meet bottleneck in many fields. There will be no making if there is no breaking. No pains no gains, we studied this in our schoolbooks when we are kids. I think a completely marketing economy must be matched up with people's risking awareness. One's life without risk can not be a wonderful life. A country without risk can just be a pool of dead water.

Then mass' confidence is the first step for the nation-wide consuming engine to restart, which can continue the growth of China's economy. I still remember a joke about Chinese people: Do you like eat or it? Eating is really a major part of Chinese people's life and I guess 90% of the consumption in the country are related to this. This is really a thing that sometimes we could do nothing about. If a folk spend more on eating we can't imagine whether people still get other needs to build another various surrounding or society. I'd say the construction of China's economy is still simplex on the fields to meet people's basic demands. Then try and innovation on new and unknown fields need to be encouraged. For this we need pioneers with great desire and selfless attitude.

Problems of the real estate is one of the reason caused the less-confident consuming. Because it occupies most of the people's soul and available capital. Housing price is always high, unbelievable higher than the mass' expectation, especially it kidnaps and deeply limits young generations' dream. It is a really big nightmare that prevents people from creating and behaviouring. It's a big burden on people's mentality and also a big stumbling block for the social development. But according to the general regulation of the marketing, someone will say it get its reasonable reason of huge demands. That's true for human's eager and desire are endless and the higher housing price is a adjuster to limit human's greediness. So this become a arguable issue and I think we still need to find solutions for this. Double-track supply in housing may solve this. Demands for common people's housing needs can mainly be fulfilled by the low-rent houses provided by government. The higher-priced commercial houses are just for market according to market rules. Hereby I wanna again mention the People's awareness is the key for this problem. In fact renting house is also an acceptable thing for common ones. We came to the world with nothing and will leave with nothing as well. Then just adjust your mentality and willingness to a mild status and you will find a very beautiful and hopeful world in front of you.

Author's points

Human being is an intelligent population on the earth and we are always looking for ways to get well along with the surroundings and get well along with one another. By using our wisdom / skills and abilities we need to make a better world for us. Sometimes consuming makes it a connection among every unit of the world. The active circulation make everything possible and then everybody can get their own chances. Risks always exist and there is a famous Chinese saying: Chasing fortunes in the danger. Then never be afraid of risk, it's part of our life and never hesitate when facing realities. Consume as you want and this helps you and helps others.